THE 100 BEST COMICS OF THE CENTURY

THE FUNNIEST CARTOONS OF ALL TIME

THE 100 BEST COMICS
OF THE CENTURY

Created by Ray Schwartz

ISBN:0-9645057-0-3

ATTENTION:
SCHOOLS AND BUSINESSES
Metropolis books are available at quantity
discounts for bulk purchase for educational,
business, or sales promotional use. For
information please write to:

Sales Department
Metropolis Publishing
3765 Motor Avenue #130
Los Angeles, California 90034

For everyone who loves to laugh

ACKNOWLEDEMENTS

We would like to Acknowledge the
invaluable assistance we received
in compiling this collection from
the *Comic Art Professional Society*
(CAPS), who helped us select the
cartoons for this book.

We would also like to thank the
following for their cooperation and
help, without them this book
would not have been possible:

Daily Features Syndicate
King Features Syndicate
Tribune Media Services
Universal Press Syndicate
United Media Services
Creators Syndicate
The National Lampoon
Omni Magazine
The Saturday Evening Post
The New Yorker Magazine
Mark Richardson Inc.
Larry Vigon
Jeanne Diamond
Sam Gross
And all the agents & cartoonists
we've worked with.

DAVE BARRY

Dave Barry was born in Armonk, New York, in 1947 and has been steadily growing older ever since without ever actually reaching maturity. Barry went to Haverford College, where he was an English major and wrote lengthy scholarly papers filled with sentences that even he did not understand. He graduated in 1969 and eventually got a job with a newspaper named - this is a real name - the "Daily Local News," in West Chester, PA, where he covered a series of incredibly dull municipal meetings, some of which are still going on.

In 1988 Barry won the Pulitzer Prize for commentary, pending a recount. His column appears in several hundred newspapers, yet another indication of the worsening drug crisis.

Barry has written a number of short but harmful books, including *Babies and Other Hazards of Sex* and *Dave Barry Slept Here; A Sort of History of the United States*. His most recent books, *Dave Barry is NOT Making This Up*, *Dave Barry Does Japan*, *Dave Barry's Only Travel Guide You'll Ever Need*, *Dave Barry Talks Back*, and *Dave Barry Turns 40* have been hailed by the critics as "containing a tremendous amount of white space."

The CBS television series "Dave's World" is based on two of Barry's books. Also, he owns a guitar that was once played by Bruce Springsteen.

Why Humor is Funny

As a professional humorist, I often get letters from readers who are interested in the basic nature of humor. "What kind of a sick, perverted, disgusting person are you," these letters typically ask, " that you make jokes about setting fire to a goat?"

And that, of course, is the wonderful thing about humor. What may seem depressing or even tragic to one person may seem like an absolute scream to another person, especially if he has had between four and seven beers. But most people agree on what is funny, and most people like to be around a person with a great sense of humor, provided he also has reasonable hygiene habits. This is why people so often ask me: "Dave, I'd like to be popular, too. How can I get a sense of humor like yours, only with less of a dependence on jokes that are primarily excuses to use the word 'booger?'

This is not an easy question. Ever since prehistoric times, wise men have tried to understand what exactly makes people laugh. That's why they were called wise men. All the other prehistoric people were out puncturing each other with spears, and the wise men were back in the cave saying: "How about: Here's my wife, please take her right now. No. How about: Would you like to take something? My wife is available. No. How about..."

Mankind didn't develop a logical system of humor until thousands of years later when Aristotle discovered, while shaving, the famous Humor Syllogism, which state, "If A is equal to B, and B is equal to C, then it would not be particularly amusing if the three of them went around poking each other in the eyes and going 'Nyuk nyuk nyuk.' At least *I* don't think it would be."

By the Elizabethan era, humor had become extremely popular. The works of Shakespeare, for example, are filled with scenes that English teachers always claim are real thigh-slappers, although when you actually decode them, it turns out they mostly depend on the use of

(continued)

(continued)

the Elizabethan word for "booger." In America today, of course, our humor is much more sophisticated, ranging all the way from television shows featuring outtakes of *commercials* where the actors can't get the words right.

If you want to develop a sense of humor of your own, you need to learn some jokes. Notice I do not say "puns." Puns are little "plays on words" that a certain breed of person loves to spring on you and then look at you in a certain self-satisfied way to indicate that he thinks that *you* must think that he is by far the cleverest person on Earth now that Benjamin Franklin is dead, when in fact what you are thinking is that if this person ever ends up in a lifeboat, the other passengers will hurl him overboard by the end of the first day even if they have plenty of food and water.

So what you want is *real* jokes. The best source for these is the authoritative *Encyclopedia Britannica* article entitled "Humor and Wit," which is in volume 99

(Humidity -Ivory Coast). This is where Carson gets all his material. It's a regular treasure trove of fun. Here's a real corker from right at the beginning:

"A masochist is a person who likes a cold shower in the morning, so he takes a hot one."

Whoooeee! That is one authoritative joke! Tell that one at a dull party, and just watch as the other guests suddenly come to life and remember important dental appointments!

But it is not enough merely to know a lot of great jokes. You also have to be able to tell them properly. Here are some tips:

1. When you tell vicious racist jokes, you should first announce that you were a liberal back when it was legal to be one.

2. Men have a certain body part that women do not have, and men always think jokes about it are a stone riot, but if you tell

such a joke to a woman, she will look at you as though you are a Baggie filled with mouse remains. I don't know why this is, but it never fails. So you want to avoid this particular type of joke in coeducational social settings such as Windsor Castle.

3. If, after you tell a joke, somebody attempts to tell you one back, you should keep assuring him that you haven't heard it, and then, when he gets to the punchline, no matter how funny it is, you should react as though he just told you the relative humidity and say: "Yeah, I heard that."

4. Never attend a large dinner party with my form mother-in-law, because she will shout across the table at you: "Tell the one about the man who's seeking the truth and he finally gets all the way to Tibet and the wise man tells him that a wet bird doesn't fly at night," and then she'll *insist* that you tell it, and then she'll tell you you told it wrong, and you might have to kill her with a fork.

INTRODUCTION

A cartoon is a single drawing or a series of drawings that makes a point or tells a joke or a story. Comic strips are a popular art form introduced into American newspapers on May 5, 1895.

Pulitzer's New York World published the first comic panel "Down Hogan's Alley" by Richard Outcault. Its central character, "The Kid," was a bald, impish tyke with a knowing grin; when, in 1896, the printer applied yellow ink to his costume, a night shirt, he became widely known as "The Yellow Kid." Outcault used the yellow shirt of one of the characters as a space to print messages, jokes, and slogans—and thus moved the written word into the picture itself. Immediately popular, these Yellow Kid panels established comics as a regular newspaper feature.

Comics have come a long way over the last one hundred years. Humor has evolved from social commentary and observations into biting sarcasm, revealing insight, and clever banter. Today's cartoons now span the gamut of humor. There are some that are so funny that they will make almost everyone laugh. So, if you are ready to have a great time, sit back and enjoy the *100 Best Comics of the Century*.

CHAOS by Brian Shuster

"Oh no, it's my husband! Quick, get back on the floor."

⑦ ROWLAND B. WILSON

Rowland B. Wilson had his first
collection of cartoons published in
1963. He has won Clio awards and
several European awards for his
work in advertising.

*"To ease your conscience as a firing squad,
one of the arrows will be a blank."*

9 CALVIN & HOBBES copyright 1986 & 1987 Watterson. Dist. by UNIVERSAL PRESS SYNDICATE. Reprinted with permission. All rights reserved.

CALVIN & HOBBES

"I SUPPOSE WHAT BOTHERS ME IS THAT IT'S THE ONE JOB WHERE YOU CAN'T SAY, 'RELAX—IT'S NOT LIKE YOU'RE PERFORMING BRAIN SURGERY.'"

13

CHIP DUNHAM

After several years of not finding one of those big bags of money that always seem to be falling out of the backs of armored cars, Chip Dunham decided he'd better get a job or something. The "or something" turned out to be cartooning. *Overboard* is Dunham's first comic strip.

OVERBOARD

7·31   Dunham

IN THE BLEACHERS

" ... And remember, we don't know how they will react to our appearance, so if you see one just stand perfectly motionless ... "

"Well, I'd like still another opinion, Doctor."

19 MIKE WILLIAMS

Mike Williams was born in
Liverpool, England. He began his
professional career by selling
cartoons to *Punch* magazine, and
he has had cartoons published in
Private Eye, *The Oldie*, *The
Spectator*, *The Times*, *Playboy* and
numerous others.

"But we'll get our sandals all muddy."

GARRY TRUDEAU

Garry Trudeau first published a cartoon called *Bull Tales* as a student at Yale University. It appeared in the college paper where it was quickly seen by newspaper syndicator Jim Andrews. Doonesbury began its national syndication in October of 1970 while Trudeau, 21 years old, was still in college.

DOONESBURY

"Bad dog!"

"Of course, it's only a prototype. The actual product will be much smaller and come in assorted fruit flavors."

29 **JACK ZIEGLER**

Jack Ziegler has been a freelance cartoonist since 1972 and a contract cartoonist for the *New Yorker* since 1974. He has published five collections of drawings.

"Oh, Margo, the pain! Will I ever get over losing you? Probably not. But that's not why I called. Is that hot-looking roommate of yours anywhere around?"

CATHY

NICK DOWNES

Nick Downes decided to become
a cartoonist after his initial career
choice, homicide detective, proved
short on laughs. He currently
supplies a wide range of magazines
and newspapers in both the U.S.
and U.K. from his residence in
Brooklyn, where he observes the
world through a high-powered
night-scope and bullet-proof glass.

'I'M SORRY YOU SAW ME TIMMY. NOW I'LL HAVE
TO KILL YOU.'

35 **DANA SUMMERS**

Dana Summers is a successful political cartoonist and comic strip creator. His incisive cartoons have appeared regularly in the *New York Times*, the *Washington Post*, *Time* and *Newsweek*. He has won awards from the Overseas Press Club and the Sigma Delta Chi Society of Professional Journalists.

BOUND & GAGGED

THE BUCKETS

"*Look, fella, I'm sorry. What more can I say?*"

"*If it please the Court, I have a get-out-of-jail-free card.*"

TOM WILSON

Ziggy, America's lovable loser, stumbled onto the comic pages in 1971 in 15 American newspapers. Two decades later, *Ziggy* appears in more than 400 newspapers with 25 million readers. Ziggy's follies and creator Tom Wilson's sensitivity to the foibles of daily life have been an inspiration to readers every day.

ZIGGY

"If payment is already in the mail, kindly disregard this notice."

GARY LARSON

Gary Larson began his cartoon career by selling six cartoons to a Seattle magazine for $90. He then developed a weekly strip called *Nature's Way* for which he was paid $3 per cartoon and which appeared in a single weekly newspaper. In 1979 the cartoon was picked-up by the *San Francisco Chronicle* just one day before Larson learned that the weekly newspaper would no longer be running it. The *Chronicle* changed the name of the cartoon to *The Far Side* and began syndicating it nationally on January 1, 1980. Larson retired on January 1, 1995.

THE FAR SIDE

By GARY LARSON

"OK, one more time and it's off to bed for the both of you. ... 'Hey, Bob. Think there are any bears in this old cave?' ... 'I dunno, Jim. Let's take a look.'"

49

MOTHER GOOSE & GRIMM

BRIAN SHUSTER

What are your earliest memories?
Well, I'm quite sure it wasn't a stork, no it was more like hummingbirds. Yes hundreds, maybe thousands, a whole swarm. I must have passed out, because the next thing I remember was being awakened by a loud slap, to find myself in the maternity ward of a Montreal hospital.

What about your education?
I went through school sequentially, starting with grade 1 and ending with a Bachelor of Arts in Communications. But my real passion was for language. I am proud to say that I speak over five HUNDRED languages. Coincidentally, most of them use the same exact words as English. But I assure you that they are, in fact, completely different languages.

Why should we read CHAOS?
Very simply, reading CHAOS helps to feed starving people, reduces pollution, eliminates poverty and disease, puts an end to all war, and closes that hole in the O-zone . . . or at least I'd like to think it does.

What else should we know about you?
I was born in 1969, moved to the U.S. when I was seven, grew up in Fresno, and went to UCLA. I created CHAOS and became an internationally syndicated cartoonist. My favorite color is aqua. I'm single, and if I had to be a tree, I would like to be an elm.

Where do you get your ideas for CHAOS?
I channel a thirteenth century comedian. You're not actually going to print that, right? I mean that just slipped out. I'm afraid that people might think I'm a little weird if they knew that I got my ideas from some guy whose been dead for 700 years. How about you just tell them that I jump up and down on my bed in my underwear until inspiration strikes.

CHAOS by Brian Shuster

"Nice and easy. I don't want to have to use this."

"Is the future clearer now or now?"

PEANUTS

"WHEN SHE SAW THE LITTLE HOUSE IN THE WOODS, SHE WONDERED WHO LIVED THERE SO SHE KNOCKED AT THE DOOR. NO ONE ANSWERED SO SHE KNOCKED AGAIN."

WHAT DO YOU THINK WILL HAPPEN?

I CAN'T IMAGINE

"...STILL NO ONE ANSWERED, SO GOLDILOCKS OPENED THE DOOR AND WALKED IN. THERE BEFORE HER, IN THE LITTLE ROOM, SHE SAW A TABLE SET FOR THREE..."

"THERE WAS A GREAT BIG BOWL OF PORRIDGE, A MIDDLE-SIZED BOWL OF PORRIDGE, AND A LITTLE, WEE BOWL OF PORRIDGE. SHE TASTED THE GREAT BIG BOWL OF PORRIDGE..."

"'OH, THIS IS TOO HOT,' SHE SAID. THEN SHE TASTED THE MIDDLE-SIZED BOWL OF PORRIDGE. 'OH, THIS IS TOO COLD.' THEN SHE TASTED THE LITTLE, WEE BOWL. 'OH, THIS IS JUST RIGHT,' SHE SAID, AND SHE ATE IT ALL UP."

I HAVE A QUESTION!

ABOUT WHAT?

WELL, IT'S IN REGARD TO COOLING...IT WOULD SEEM TO ME THAT IF THE MIDDLE-SIZED BOWL WAS COLD, THE LITTLE, WEE BOWL WOULD BE COLD, TOO, RATHER THAN 'JUST RIGHT,' AND..

POW!

I NEVER EVEN BROUGHT UP THE FAR MORE OBVIOUS POINT OF UNLAWFUL ENTRY!

"Oh, go ahead and swallow it. Does everything you eat have to have a name?"

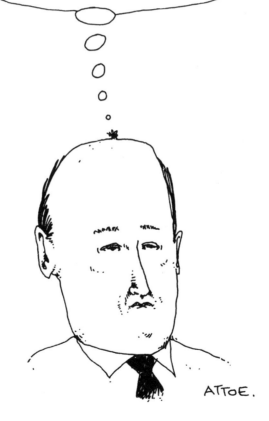

"Don't forget, the satellite photo man will be watching you!"

63 **BILL WATTERSON**

Bill Watterson was born in 1958 and raised in Chagrin Falls, Ohio. Upon graduation from college he became a political cartoonist for the *Cincinnati Post*. Watterson began creating ideas for comic strips in 1980, and Calvin and Hobbes began their existence as background characters for a cartoon strip that was never published. When a strip was created that featured the pair, however, it was purchased by a major syndicate, and *Calvin and Hobbes* began appearing in newspapers everywhere.

CALVIN AND HOBBES

DILBERT

THAT'S RIGHT ... COUGH-
COUGH! ... I WON'T BE IN
TO WORK ... COUGH-WHEEZE-
COUGH ...

BAD COLD? WELL, NO,
ACTUALLY I HAVE A BAD
HEADACHE ...

BUT I DON'T KNOW
HOW TO MAKE A
HEADACHE SOUND OVER
THE PHONE.

S. Adams

12-18

69 ROZ CHAST

Roz Chast was born in Brooklyn,
New York. She graduated from
Rhode Island School of Design in
1977 with a BFA in Painting. Her
cartoons have appeared in *The New
Yorker* since 1978.

"... and a side order of fries."

73

JIM DAVIS

Jim Davis grew up on a small farm with 25 cats. When asthma forced him inside, away form his regular farm chores, the young Davis spent hours drawing. After college, Davis joined *Tumbleweeds* creator Tom Ryan as his cartoon assistant. Davis noticed that there were numerous comic strips about dogs but few about cats, even though the world is full of cat lovers. Garfield, a fat, lazy, lasagna-loving, cynical cat became a formula for his success that led to the syndication of *Garfield* in 1978.

GARFIELD

CHAOS by Brian Shuster

"I know it's a long shot, but heck, he already has a pair of horses."

GAHAN WILSON

Gahan Wilson is descended from such authentic American folk heroes as circus king, P.T. Barnum and silver-voiced orator, William Jennings Bryan. He was officially declared born dead but rescued by a doctor who dipped him alternately in bowls of hot and cold water. He became the first student in The Art Institute of Chicago to actually admit he was going there to learn how to become a cartoonist.

"First, let me put your mind at ease about that being a hallucination. . . ."

"An interesting phenomenon...the weakest and least intelligent male seems to have developed a system of taxation."

FRANK AND ERNEST ®by Bob Thaves

ANYPLACE BUT CALIFORNIA — THE LAST TIME WE LANDED THERE WE STARTED SIX RELIGIONS.

© 1987 by NEA, Inc.   THAVES 5-16

GET RICH QUICK SCHEMES
$ 1,000,000 EACH

SCHWADRon

HELLO! WE'RE GIANT COCKROACHES FROM ANOTHER DIMENSION, AND DON'T ASK US WHY, BUT WE'D LIKE TO SEE YOUR TOASTER!

© 1986 Universal Press Syndicate

WATTERSON

4-13

"Bad news . . . We've been ordered to stop work on the new mall."

95 **J.B. HANDELSMAN**

J.B. Handelsman was born in
New York City. He has
contributed to *Playboy*, *The New
Yorker*, and *Punch* magazines.

"So far, they haven't objected to my using their name, and you'd be amazed how much insurance I'm selling."

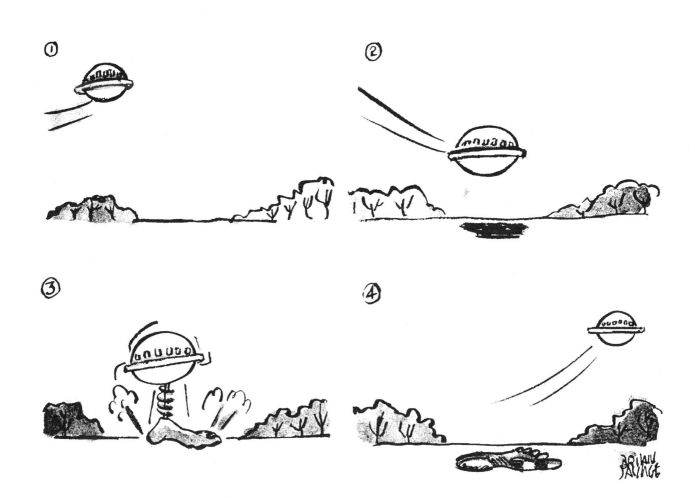

BERKELEY BREATHED

99

Berkeley Breathed began his career in 1977 by drawing a political cartoon and submitting it to the University of Texas Daily Texan. In 1980, *Bloom County* was nationally syndicated and quickly became one of the most popular comic strips of the 1980s. In 1987, Breathed won a Pulitzer Prize for distinguished cartooning.

BLOOM COUNTY

"Hello, Rover's Retreat, formerly known as the Acme Obedience School."

ED SUBITZKY

"Discovered" by the staff of *National Lampoon* magazine in 1973, Ed Subitzky has been on the masthead for twenty years. He is probably best known for his Lampoon comic strips, cartoons and humor articles. Not the least of his accomplishments have been twelve appearances on the Late Night With David Letterman show.

HYPNO-COMICS! by ED SUBITZKY

PUTS YOU IN A TRANCE!

... AND NOW THAT I HAVE SNAPPED MY FINGERS, YOU HAVE BLANKED OUT EVERYTHING YOU JUST READ!

THE END

105 MIKE PETERS

Mike Peters began drawing as a young child. His cartoons began appearing weekly at the early age of 15. Peters became an editorial cartoonist before developing *Mother Goose & Grimm*.

MOTHER GOOSE & GRIMM

OF COURSE,, IF YOU CAN'T AFFORD OUR **BRICK** BOMB SHELTER, WE DO HAVE ONE MADE OF **STRAW**!!!

CHAOS by Brian Shuster

"Just kidding Al, it's me, Dr. Hanks!"

109 **JOE KOHL**

Joe Kohl is a nationally renowned
cartoonist. His cartoons have
appeared in many national
magazines, such as *Good
Housekeeping*, *The National
Enquirer* and *National Lampoon*,
and in numerous books and
greeting cards.

" 'Better or worse' and 'richer or poorer' are not 'choices.' "

DILBERT

I BOUGHT A PHONE ANSWERING MACHINE.

WAS THE PHONE ASKING YOU QUESTIONS YOU COULDN'T ANSWER ON YOUR OWN?

12-17

THE HARD PART IS THINKING OF A GREETING MESSAGE.

© 1989 United Feature Syndicate, Inc.

"HI. THIS IS DILBERT. I'M NOT HERE RIGHT NOW."

"WELL, TECHNICALLY I AM HERE 'NOW'..."

"BUT 'NOW' IS A RELATIVE TERM, SO USE YOUR BEST JUDGMENT IN DECIDING WHETHER I'M HERE."

HMM...THAT WAS ACTUALLY A CREATIVE LITTLE MESSAGE.

DEMONSTRATING, ONCE AGAIN, THAT SUBTLE DIFFERENCE BETWEEN CREATIVITY AND COMPLEX STUPIDITY.

S.Adams

GEORGE TROSLEY

George Trosley was graduated
from the Hussian School of Art in
Philadelphia. In 1973 he jumped
into cartooning full-time and has
been delivering laughs on paper
ever since. His work has appeared
in *Saturday Evening Post, National
Enquirer, Saturday Review, Hustler*
and many other publications.

"Okay. Anything from the top shelf."

115 **CHRISTOPHER BROWNE**

Christopher Browne has had his
work published all over, including,
of course, *Playboy* Magazine.

CRUISER

Christopher Browne

117 **NURIT KARLIN**

Nurit Karlin was born and grew up in Jerusalem, Israel. She lives and works in New York. She has published cartoons and illustrations in many major magazines and contributes regularly to the *Wall Street Journal*, the *Washington Post* and the *New York Times*.

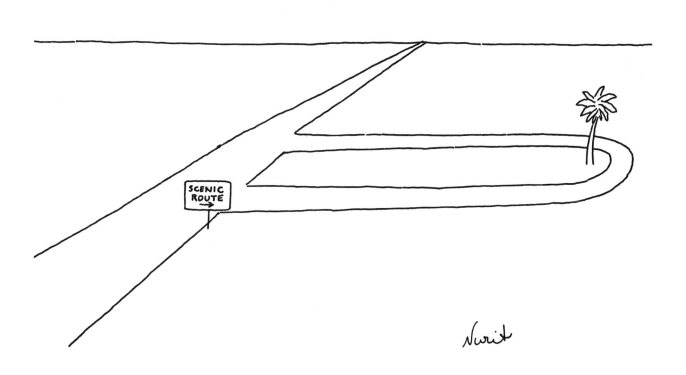

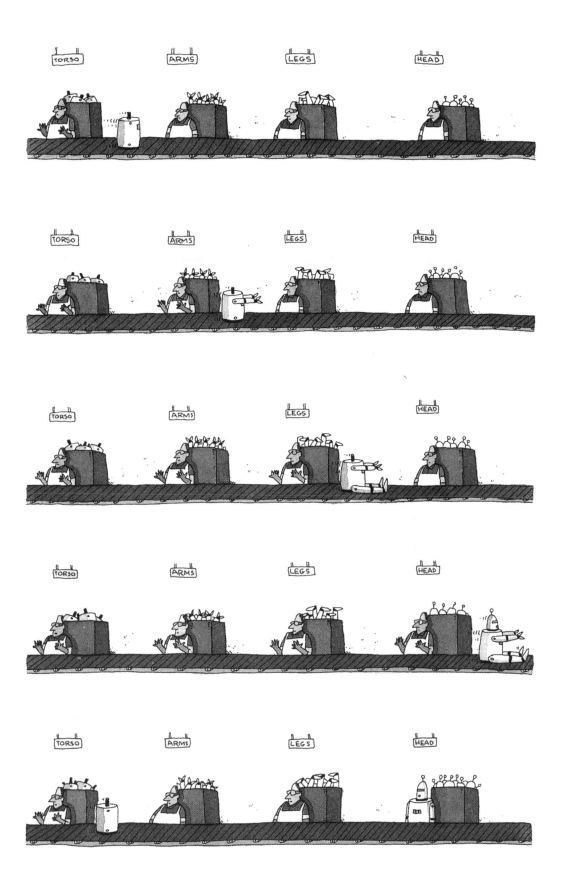

B. "HAP" KLIBAN

Kliban was born, January 1, 1935, in Norwalk, Connecticut. He heard about a new magazine that was interested in buying cartoons and sold his first cartoon to *Playboy*. Kliban has also sold to the *New Yorker*, *National Lampoon*, *Esquire*, and *Punch*. B. Kliban died in 1990, but the breadth of his work, much of it currently unpublished, will continue as a durable testament to his monumental craft.

BKliban© ©1976

MOVIE CRITICS ON OTHER PLANETS

I'LL HAVE A BONE, A CAT, AND A TENNIS BALL!

BILL AMEND

Fox Trot is a comic strip where the characters have real personality. The humor and appeal derive from the interaction of its characters. Surprise is the base of all humor, and nothing is more surprising than the truth. *Fox Trot* has the ring of truth to it.

FOX TROT

"WATCH THE NEW GUY. I DON'T TRUST HIM."

"It would look better over there."

137

CATHY GUISEWITE

Cathy Guisewite gives a delightfully funny yet honest look at the single career woman's life in the nineties. *Cathy*, the character who has given a voice to the anxieties and triumphs of modern women, appears in more than 900 daily and Sunday newspapers worldwide.

CATHY

SID HARRIS

Sidney Harris is the resident funny man of science. He has been a frequent contributor of cartoons to *Current Contents*, *American Scientist*, *Discover*, *Science 85*, *Datamation*, *Physics Today*, and *Medical Economics*, as well as to the *New Yorker*, *Playboy*, *Wall Street Journal*, *National Lampoon*, *Punch*, *Chicago Magazine*, and the *Washingtonian*. A freelance cartoonist for more than twenty-five years, Harris has published six books of cartoons.

"I THINK YOU SHOULD BE MORE EXPLICIT HERE IN STEP TWO."

the WIZARD of ID

by Brant parker and Johnny hart

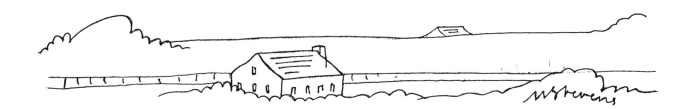

"We know what happens to bad little boys who won't
eat their cereal, don't we?"

151 **STEVE MOORE**

Steve Moore, who began cartooning at age fourteen in his eighth-grade English textbook, lives in Marina Del Rey, California. When his is not holding down the news editor's desk at the *Los Angeles Times*, Steve gets many of his best ideas for his cartoons while stuck in Southern California freeway traffic.

Naismith invents "Basket," the unsuccessful forerunner to the game of basketball.

PEANUTS

"IT'S MY EARS, DOC. I CAN'T MOVE THEM. THEY'RE...THEY'RE PARALYZED."

BOB THAVES

Bob Thaves' single-panel comic strip features Frank and Ernest. These characters have the ability to appear as any person, place or thing in any time period, past, present, or future. *Frank & Ernest* is distributed to more than 1,200 newspapers worldwide. Thaves has been honored with three Reuben Awards for Best Syndicated Panel in 1983, 1984 and 1986.

FRANK AND ERNEST

by Bob Thaves

163 SAM GROSS

Sam Gross' cartoons appear
regularly in *The New Yorker*,
Playboy and *National Lampoon*.
His work has been compiled into
several books, including *I Am
Blind and My Dog is Dead* and *More
Gross*, and he has edited several
cartoon collections, including *Cats
Cats Cats*, *Food Food Food*, and
Golf Golf Golf.

165

MISTER BOFFO
by Joe Martin

Shanahan

SCOTT ADAMS

Scott Adams' *Dilbert* is read by more than 30 million people every day through more than 260 newspapers worldwide. *Dilbert* has been syndicated since 1989, and it was the first comic strip available on the Internet.

DILBERT reprinted by permission of UFS, Inc.

DILBERT

WHEN I STARTED PROGRAMMING, WE DIDN'T HAVE ANY OF THESE SISSY "ICONS" AND "WINDOWS."

ALL WE HAD WERE ZEROS AND ONES -- AND SOMETIMES WE DIDN'T EVEN HAVE ONES.

9-8

I WROTE AN ENTIRE DATABASE PROGRAM USING ONLY ZEROS.

YOU HAD ZEROS? WE HAD TO USE THE LETTER "O."

"THOSE ARE THE LAWS, MOSES... NOW GO FORTH AND OPEN LAW OFFICES IN CONVENIENT LOCATIONS."

175 **RUSSELL MYERS**

Away from the drawing board, Russell Myers is as disappointingly businesslike as a small-town hardware dealer. "Contrary to popular opinion," he once told a magazine writer, "to quote Gaylord Buzzard who quoted me, I do not have the first dollar I ever owned. However, I do have the name and address of its second owner." *Broom-Hilda* began publication on April 19, 1970.

BROOM-HILDA

"I don't think it's to do with your begetting an infant prodigy, Dad, so much as it's to do with you being stupid."

"WHAT WAS THE NAME OF THAT OBEDIENCE SCHOOL?"

181 CHARLES BARSOTTI

Charles Barsotti began his cartoon career by freelancing for *The New Yorker* and the *Saturday Evening Post*. He had a daily cartoon which ran in *USA Today* for eight years. His work has also appeared in the *Atlantic*, *The New York Times*, *Punch*, *Playboy*, *Texas Monthly*, *Discover*, *The Kansas City Star* and others.

"It's a fried telephone book! We gave it a fancy French name and you ordered it!"

183 DIK BROWNE

Dik Browne created *Hagar the Horrible* in the laundry room of his Connecticut home. Launched in 1973, *Hagar* is now syndicated to more than 1,800 newspapers around the world, a circulation achieved by fewer than 10 strips in the entire history of the art form. Browne died June 4, 1989 after a long battle with cancer, and his two sons have since been producing the comic.

HÄGAR the Horrible
®
By Dik Browne

WILEY

For Wiley, his comic strip *Non Sequitur* is the culmination of a decade and a half of award-winning cartooning. It was named best comic strip of 1992 by the National Cartoonists Society. Wiley says, "My approach is ridiculously simple: Produce the funniest, best-drawn cartoon possible, regardless of theme, subject matter or setting."

NON SEQUITUR

"I've got a date tonight, Mom.
Can I borrow the bag?"

IMMEDIATELY AFTER ORVILLE WRIGHT'S HISTORIC 12-SECOND FLIGHT, HIS LUGGAGE COULD NOT BE LOCATED.

MOTHER GOOSE & GRIMM

"I give up, Robert. What does have two horns, one eye, and creeps?"

"And just what are you planning to do with your silly, intergalactic, demolecularizing time-traveling module?"

201   **RICH TENNANT**

For the past seven years, cartoonist Rich Tennant has been recording the proliferation of computers through his cartoon series *The 5th Wave*. His work has appeared in corporate newsletters and magazines including Xerox, IBM Canada, Lotus Development, Price Waterhouse, Compaq Computer as well as *PC Magazine*, and *Computerworld*.

The 5th Wave

By Rich Tennant

"NAAAH—HE'S NOT THAT SMART. HE WON'T BACK UP HIS HARD DISK, FORGETS TO CONSISTENTLY NAME HIS FILES, AND DROOLS ALL OVER THE KEYBOARD."

CHARLES M. SCHULZ

"It seems beyond the comprehension of people that someone can be born to draw comic strips, but I think I was," says Charles M. Schulz creator of *Peanuts*. "My ambition from earliest memory was to produce a daily comic strip." And that is exactly what Schulz has done every day since *Peanuts* debuted in seven newspapers on October 2, 1950. Schulz's first break came in 1947 when he sold a cartoon feature called "Li'l Folks" to the *St. Paul Pioneer Press*. More than 40 years later, *Peanuts* appears in 2,400 newspapers worldwide and Charles M. Schulz has become a household name.

PEANUTS

by Schulz

Request for submissions:

If you have a cartoon that you think should be included in our next book because it makes you really laugh, then send us a copy, along with any information about the cartoonist and where you found the cartoon. If we publish it in a future edition, you will receive a finders fee*. Send your submissions to:

Metropolis Publishing
3765 Motor Avenue #130
Los Angeles Califronia 90034.

*Some restrictions apply.

If you would like to be on our Preferred List and receive special FREE advance notices of future Metropolis books, as well as special discounts, just send us the attached post card. Please print.

Cut on dotted line

Name

Address

City   State

Zip   Phone

PLACE
FIRST
CLASS
POSTAGE
HERE

Metropolis Publishing
3765 Motor Avenue #130
Los Angeles, California 90034